One Direction

ABDO
Publishing Company

Big Buddy BOOKS
Buddy Bios

by **Sarah Tieck**

VISIT US AT
www.abdopublishing.com

Published by ABDO Publishing Company, PO Box 398166, Minneapolis, Minnesota 55439.

Copyright © 2013 by Abdo Consulting Group, Inc. International copyrights reserved in all countries. No part of this book may be reproduced in any form without written permission from the publisher. Big Buddy Books™ is a trademark and logo of ABDO Publishing Company.

Printed in the United States of America, North Mankato, Minnesota.
102012
012014
PRINTED ON RECYCLED PAPER

Coordinating Series Editor: Rochelle Baltzer
Contributing Editors: Stephanie Hedlund, Marcia Zappa
Graphic Design: Maria Hosley
Cover Photograph: *AP Photo*: Luca Bruno.
Interior Photographs/Illustrations: *AP Photo*: Evan Agostini/Invision (p. 21), Andreas Branch/PatrickMcMullan.com/ Sipa USA (Sipa via AP Images) (p. 5), Katie Collins/PA Wire URN:9705456 (Press Association via AP Images) (p. 7), Owen Humphreys/PA Wire. EDITORIAL USE ONLY URN:14296506 (Press Association via AP Images) (p. 25), John Marshall JME (p. 13), Yui Mok/PA Wire URN:9894605 (Press Association via AP Images) (p. 7), PA Wire URN:14081391 (Press Association via AP Images) (p. 27), Rex Features via AP Images (pp. 9, 17); *Getty Images*: Jo Hale (p. 23), Hagen Hopkins (p. 11), Keystone (p. 11), Peter Kramer/NBC/NBC NewsWire via Getty Images (p. 15), Jason LaVeris/FilmMagic (p. 29), Ben Pruchnie/Getty Images for Westfield (p. 19), Taro Yamasaki/Time Life Pictures (p. 11).

Cataloging-in-Publication Data

Tieck, Sarah.
  One Direction: popular boy band / Sarah Tieck.
    p. cm. -- (Big buddy biographies)
  ISBN 978-1-61783-752-4
  1. One Direction (Musical group)--Juvenile literature. 2. Rock musicians--England--Biography--Juvenile literature.
I. Title.
  782.42164092/2--dc22
  [B]
                    2012946544

One Direction

Contents

Rising Stars

One Direction is a music group. Its members sing popular music. They are Niall Horan, Zayn Malik, Liam Payne, Harry Styles, and Louis Tomlinson. Fans around the world enjoy their songs!

Louis, Zayn, Niall, Harry, and Liam (*left to right*) make up One Direction.

Where in the World?

ATLANTIC OCEAN

Scotland

NORTH SEA

Northern Ireland

UNITED KINGDOM

IRELAND

Wales

England
London

Starting Out

One Direction formed in London, England, in 2010. Its members started out as **solo performers** on *The X Factor*. Before long, they were cut from the show.

But, the judges thought they would make a good singing group. So, the boys stayed on the show. They worked together as a group called One Direction. Soon, they had many fans!

Judge Simon Cowell (*third from right*) helped the boys grow into a group. He is known for his knowledge of the music business.

During *The X Factor*, the boys lived together. They grew close!

Did you know...

The X Factor is a television show that started in the United Kingdom. On the show, singers compete for a recording contract.

First Album

One Direction took third place on *The X Factor*. Soon after, the group was asked to record an album. The boys spent many hours practicing and recording songs for it.

In 2011, One Direction **released** *Up All Night*. It became a hit in the United Kingdom! Soon, people in the United States and other countries noticed their music.

Fan Fever

Over the years, many bands have become very popular. These include the Beatles, New Kids on the Block, and Jonas Brothers. Like these bands, One Direction has very excited fans!

One Direction has gained many fans quickly through **social media**. Fans around the world use social media to share photos and videos of the band. And, the band uses it to send messages to fans.

The Beatles became popular in the 1960s. New Kids on the Block became popular in the 1980s. Beatles fans (*left*) and New Kids on the Block fans (*below*) were very excited to see the bands!

People learned about One Direction on the Internet. This helped them become popular very quickly in the United States and Europe.

Big Break

Up All Night was very popular! Its first hit song was "What Makes You Beautiful." Its other hit songs include "Gotta Be You" and "One Thing."

The band members are also authors. They wrote *One Direction: Forever Young: Our Official X Factor Story*. This book is about becoming a band. Later, they wrote *One Direction: Dare to Dream: Life as One Direction*.

In 2012, One Direction won a BRIT Award for "What Makes You Beautiful."

Irish Eyes

The members of One Direction did not know each other before *The X Factor*. Niall James Horan was born in Mullingar, Ireland, on September 13, 1993. His parents are Maura Gallagher and Bobby Horan. They divorced when Niall was five.

Niall has always loved music. He learned to play the recorder at school. When he was about 12, he learned to play the **guitar**. He later joined the school choir. Before *The X Factor*, he planned to study sound **engineering** in college.

Niall is the group's only Irish member.
He speaks with an Irish accent.

The Quiet One

Zain Javadd "Zayn" Malik was born in Bradford, England, on January 12, 1993. His parents are Yaser and Tricia Malik. Zayn is part Irish, English, and Pakistani.

Young Zayn loved singing, painting, and drawing. And even though he was quiet, he liked acting.

When Zayn was about 15, his music teacher suggested that he try out for *The X Factor*. At age 17, he did. But, he almost didn't **audition**. His mom pushed him to do it!

Zayn has many tattoos with special meanings. Some mean good luck. He has his grandfather's name tattooed on his chest.

Big Voice

Liam James Payne was born in Wolverhampton, England, on August 29, 1993. His parents are Karen and Geoff Payne. From the time he was a baby, Liam was often sick. When he was a child, he had many health problems.

Liam always loved singing and dancing. At age 14, he tried out for *The X Factor* to meet Simon. He didn't make it to the finals. But, he practiced his skills. At 16, he **auditioned** again. This time, he found success!

Did you know...

Liam is a talented runner. He was on the reserve list for the 2012 London Olympics!

19

The Funny One

Harry Edward Styles was born in Holmes Chapel, England, on February 1, 1994. His parents are Des Styles and Ann Cox. They divorced when Harry was seven.

Growing up, Harry enjoyed math and English. He also liked playing soccer. Harry acted in school plays and sang at home for fun. In high school, he formed a band with friends. But, he never guessed he'd be part of a famous boy band!

IMAX 3D

Did you know...

Harry came up with the band's name.

Wild Card

Louis William Tomlinson was born in Doncaster, England, on December 24, 1991. His mother is Johannah Tomlinson.

From a young age, Louis liked making people laugh. As a teenager, he did some acting on television. And, he joined a band called the Rogue.

In 2009, Louis tried out for *The X Factor*. He didn't make it. But, he kept practicing. He **auditioned** again in 2010. This time, he made it!

Louis likes to shop and is known for his crazy clothes.

A Musical Life

The members of One Direction spend many hours practicing and recording music. They also go on tour and perform live concerts.

When they are on tour, Niall, Zayn, Liam, Harry, and Louis may spend months away from home. They travel to cities around the world. They also attend events and meet fans. Their fans are always excited to see them!

In 2012, One Direction performed at the Olympic Games.

Off the Stage

The members of One Direction often spend free time at home. They visit their friends and family. And, they enjoy playing games and watching TV.

The group also likes to help people in need. Sometimes, the boys help raise money for certain causes.

In 2012, the members of One Direction helped a charity called Flying Start. They served food and drinks on a special flight to raise money for children in need.

One Direction sang "One Thing" at the 2012 MTV Video Music Awards.

Buzz

One Direction's opportunities continue to grow. The band **released** its second album in 2012. It is called *Take Me Home*. Fans are excited to see what the group will sing and write next!

Did you know...

One Direction's music has been used for television shows. In 2012, the band appeared on *iCarly*.

Snapshot

★**Names**: Niall James Horan; Zain Javadd "Zayn" Malik; Liam James Payne; Harry Edward Styles; Louis William Tomlinson

★**Birthdays**: September 13, 1993 (Niall); January 12, 1993 (Zayn); August 29, 1993 (Liam); February 1, 1994 (Harry); December 24, 1991 (Louis)

★**Albums**: *Up All Night, Take Me Home*

Important Words

audition (aw-DIH-shuhn) to give a trial performance showcasing personal talent as a musician, a singer, a dancer, or an actor.

engineering (ehn-juh-NIHR-ihng) applying scientific knowledge to a practical purpose such as building machines or buildings.

guitar (guh-TAHR) a stringed musical instrument played by strumming.

perform to do something in front of an audience.

release to make available to the public.

social media a form of communication on the Internet where people can share information, messages, and videos. It may include blogs and online groups.

solo a performance by a single person.

Web Sites

To learn more about One Direction, visit ABDO Publishing Company online. Web sites about One Direction are featured on our Book Links page. These links are routinely monitored and updated to provide the most current information available.

www.abdopublishing.com

Index